POOP

A (Very) Natural History & A Powerful Future

For everyone who, like me, secretly thinks
poo is the most amazing stuff.
BH

For Amy and Sammy, who are such good company
while I draw. Lots of love, Jenny
JNRS

Poop: A (Very) Natural History & A Powerful Future © 2025 Quarto Publishing plc.
Text © 2025 Ben Hoare. Illustrations © 2025 Jennifer NR Smith.

First Published in 2025 by Wide Eyed Editions,
an imprint of The Quarto Group.
100 Cummings Center, Suite 265D, Beverly, MA 01915, USA.
T (978) 282-9590 F (978) 283-2742 www.Quarto.com

The right of Jennifer N. R. Smith to be identified as the illustrator and Ben Hoare to
be identified as the author of this work has been asserted by them in accordance
with the Copyright, Designs and Patents Act, 1988 (United Kingdom).

All rights reserved.

No part of this publication may be reproduced, stored in a retrieval system, or
transmitted, in any form, or by any means, electrical, mechanical, photocopying,
recording or otherwise without the prior written permission of the publisher or a
licence permitting restricted copying.

A catalogue record for this book is available from the British Library.

ISBN 978-0-71129-449-3

The illustrations were created digitally
Set in Lust and Futura

Designer: Myrto Dimitrakoulia
Editor: Corinne Lucas and Hollie Cayzer
Production Controller: Dawn Cameron
Art Director: Karissa Santos
Publisher: Debbie Foy

Manufactured in Guangdong, China TT202505

9 8 7 6 5 4 3 2 1

POOP

A (Very) Natural History
& A Powerful Future

Ben Hoare
Jennifer N. R. Smith

WIDE EYED EDITIONS

Contents

Where There's Life, There's Poop.	6
Poop and You	8
What Goes into Poop?	10
The Wild Journey Inside You	12
The Grand Finale	16
The Truth About Pees, Farts, and Burps	18
Poop and Health	20
It Takes Guts	22
Time to Come Clean	24
Poop Pitfalls	26
Poop Potions	28
The Stuff of Life	30
Calls of Nature	32
Poop Parade	34
The Surprising Feast in the Animal Kingdom	36
Too Good to Waste	38

Poop Through the Ages — **40**
    Bathroom Breaks — **42**
    Flush With Success — **46**
    Making Money From Muck — **48**
    The Great Stink — **50**
    A Gift That Keeps on Giving — **52**

Poop Planet — **54**
    Poop to the Rescue — **56**
    Building Blocks — **58**
    Rescuing the River — **60**
    Can Poop Save the World? — **62**

The Science of Poop — **64**
    Blue Poop Challenge — **66**
    Every Poop Tells a Story — **68**
    Space Poop Odyssey — **70**

Whose Poop? — **72**
Poop Knew — **76**

Glossary — **78**

Index — **80**

Where There's Life, There's Poop.

Poop, feces, excrement—it goes by many names, and let's face it, many people find it disgusting. You might catch someone cracking a joke about how stinky the stuff is. But I'm about to let you in on a little secret: poop is wonderful. I'm not kidding, poop really is one of the most amazing materials on Earth!

For starters, poop doesn't always look the same. It can come in different colors like blue or pink! Poop can also be incredibly useful. Did you know it can be turned into beautiful paper? And some of the delicious foods we eat are probably grown using poop! We can even use poop to create electricity and save lives. But it's not just humans who benefit from poop. Many animals, from beetles to whales, need it to survive. Some of them even have it for dinner!

Of course, we don't need to pick up poop to learn about it. Doctors and scientists can study it to understand what it tells us about our health. And we can learn a lot about its history and significance in our lives without getting our hands dirty.

So, are you ready to become a poop expert? Let's explore the human digestive system to find out how we make poop, what it is, and what happens to it afterward. We'll also learn about animal poop, meet an ancient god of poop and see how poop is essential to the future of life on this planet!

See, I told you poop is awesome stuff.

Poop and You

Our bodies produce poop most days, but what even *is* poop? Most people think it's just the leftover stuff from the food we eat. While that's partially true, there's a lot more to it than that! When we eat a meal, our body breaks it down and takes out all the useful parts to use as energy. The rest is waste and exits our body as poop.

Your body works hard to make poop. Many organs team up to get the job done, and they all have different things to do. This amazing team is called the digestive system. In a moment, we'll see it in action.

And talking about poop wouldn't be complete without mentioning pee, farts, and burps, right?
So, let's find out what those are too!

What Goes into Poop?

Every poop you take is a mixture of waste from your body.
Let's dive into the world of human poop and see what goes into making one!

Liquid wonders

Did you know that poop is made of around seventy-five percent water? That might sound surprising, but your body doesn't just get rid of water when you pee, it also says goodbye to water when you poop. The rest of the poop is solid stuff...

Bacteria bonanza

The human body is full of bacteria and some end up in your poop. Some of these bacteria are alive and some are dead. There are around 100 billion bacteria rocking around in every gram of your poop!

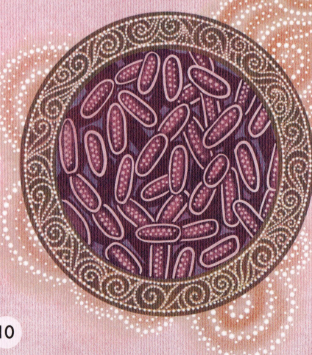

Poop parade

Get ready for a parade of dead cells! Every day, billions of your cells die and end up in your poop. Most of them are old red blood cells that release a brown chemical called bilirubin (bil–ee–roo–bin) which gives poop its brown color.

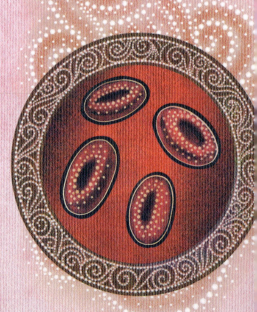

Fiber fiesta

Meet fiber—a tough substance found in plant foods, such as wholegrains, nuts, beans, fruit, and vegetables. Your body can't digest fiber, so it passes straight into your poop. Fiber is super-important because it makes your poop solid and speeds up its journey through your body.

HAVE YOU EVER EATEN SWEETCORN OR CORN ON THE COB AND SEEN THE YELLOW KERNELS APPEAR IN YOUR POOP? THE REASON IS THEY'RE SO FULL OF FIBER YOUR BODY CAN'T BREAK THEM DOWN, SO THEY GO STRAIGHT THROUGH YOUR GUT!

Brilliant bile

Finally, your poop contains a little bile. This is a green-yellow liquid made by your liver, and its job is to break down the fat in your food.

Tasty adventures

Ever heard the saying, "You are what you eat"? Well it's true! You really are built from the food you eat. And to keep your body feeling fabulous, here's a secret: try eating lots of different types of foods every week! This is what we call a "balanced diet," and it's a wonderful way to have healthy pooping habits.

Quirky quest

Various other things that your body can't digest or no longer needs also go into your poop. They include fats, proteins, and minerals.

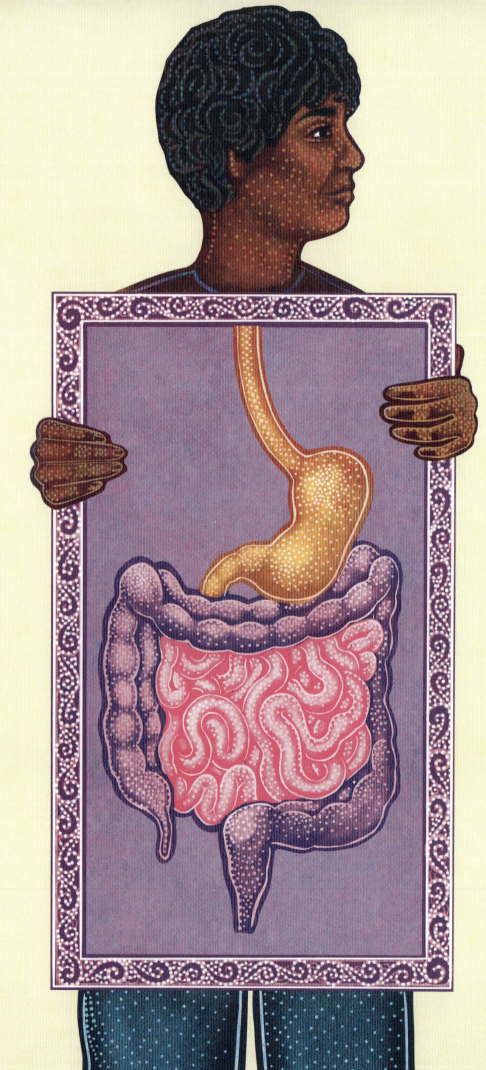

The Wild Journey Inside You

Have you ever thought about what happens to your favorite sandwich after you take a big bite? Well, get ready for an incredible journey through your body—it's called digestion!

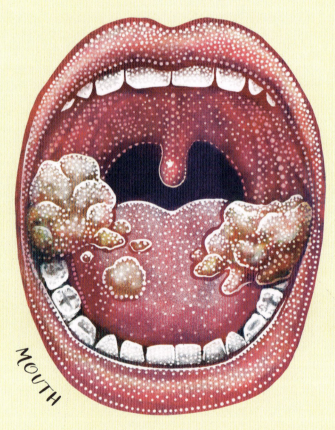

MOUTH

The adventure begins in your mouth, with the first bite of the sandwich. As you chew, your teeth crush and mash the bread and filling. Your spit, or saliva, makes everything wet and mushy so that it's easier to swallow. Your spit also begins the process of digestion, by breaking down some of the carbohydrates in the food and turning them into sugars. Look in a mirror and open your mouth. The half-chewed mess you can see is the start of the digestion process!

When you swallow, the ball of food slips down your throat and enters a narrow tube called the esophagus (ee-sof-uh-gus). This tube winds its way down into your chest, past your ribs, heart, and lungs. But the food doesn't just fall—powerful muscles contract and push it down.

IN ADULTS, FOOD TRAVELS OVER 30 FEET FROM THEIR MOUTH TO THEIR BUM. IN CHILDREN, FOOD DOES NOT HAVE TO TRAVEL QUITE AS FAR, BUT IT STILL HAS A WILD RIDE!

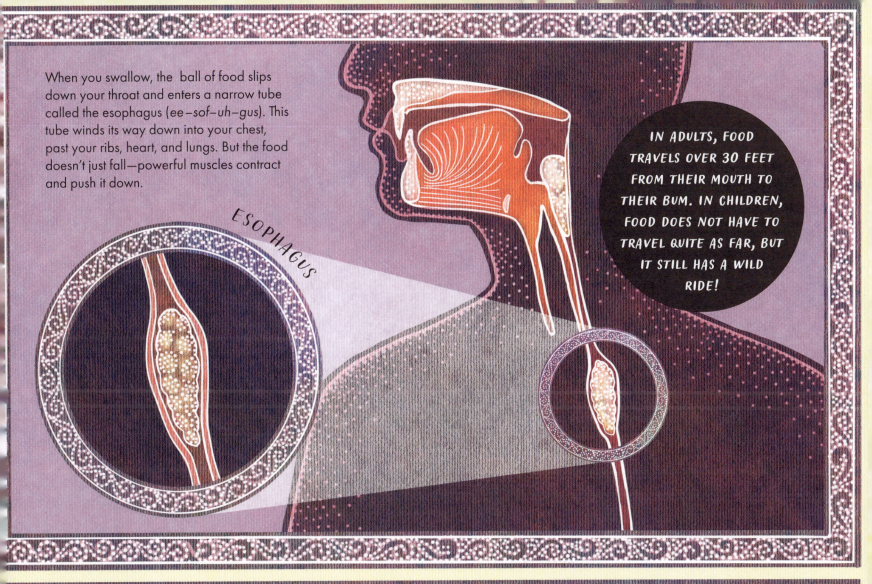

Next stop – your stomach! This muscular bag is where things really kick off. It churns the food into a soupy mixture and unleashes its super-strong acid, which can dissolve metal! This acid also kills off any bacteria that might be lurking in your food. (The awful taste that vomit leaves in your mouth is from the stomach acid!)

The soupy mixture stays there for about an hour or two, or sometimes a little longer. But where does it go next? If you think it's going straight to becoming poop, well, that would be skipping ahead a bit. Actually, the sloppy remains of the sandwich are *nowhere near* ready to be made into poop yet, because your stomach is *not* where most digestion happens.

Digestion mainly takes place in your small intestine. And this huge organ is the next stop on the food's rollercoaster ride...

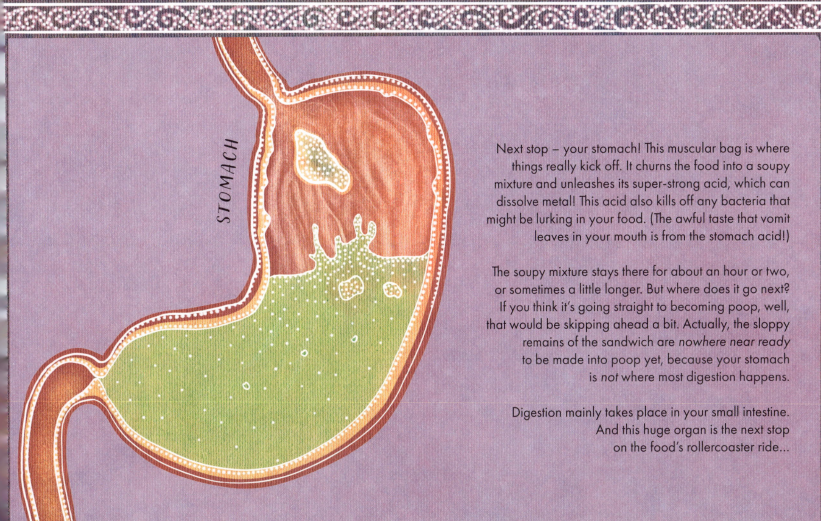

Straight after leaving your stomach, the slop that was once your tasty sandwich arrives at your small intestine. This is where the real digestive action takes place.

Contrary to its name, the small intestine is the largest organ in your digestive system. What's left of the sandwich takes six to eight hours to travel through all the winding tubes of the small intestine. It's not an easy journey, as the narrow tubes require a lot of effort to push the food forward. Thankfully, the small intestine is armed with strong muscles that squeeze and push the sloppy food through its winding passages.

Your small intestine is a master at extracting nutrients from the food, including carbohydrates, proteins, fats, and other essential elements. Your blood absorbs these nutrients and whisks them away for your body to use. All that remains of your sandwich is a murky liquid...

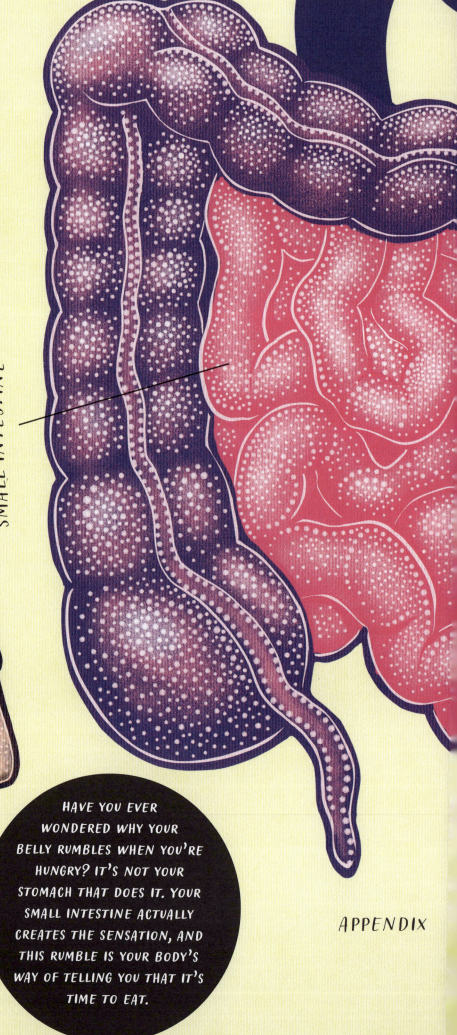

SMALL INTESTINE

APPENDIX

HAVE YOU EVER WONDERED WHY YOUR BELLY RUMBLES WHEN YOU'RE HUNGRY? IT'S NOT YOUR STOMACH THAT DOES IT. YOUR SMALL INTESTINE ACTUALLY CREATES THE SENSATION, AND THIS RUMBLE IS YOUR BODY'S WAY OF TELLING YOU THAT IT'S TIME TO EAT.

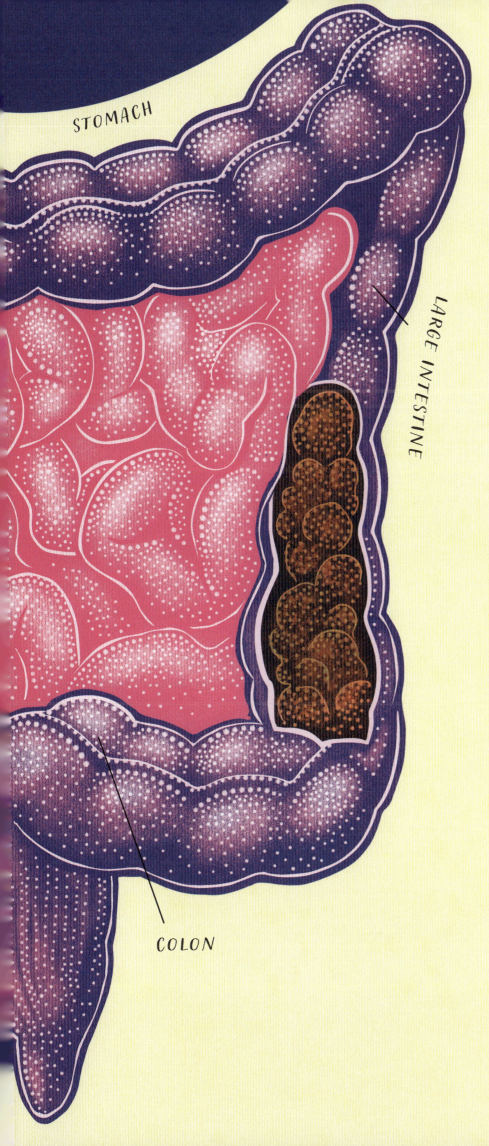

STOMACH

LARGE INTESTINE

COLON

FRIENDLY BACTERIA

Next stop—the large intestine. It is here, in the long and squiggly section called the colon, that the liquid starts turning into poop. The colon removes some of the water from the liquid, which your body uses for other things. As this water is removed, the waste material becomes more solid and poop-like. Your colon is home to trillions of friendly bacteria that interact with the poop and remove any nutrients missed by the small intestine, including vitamins, and pass them on to your body to use. Thanks, bacteria!

Your colon needs around twelve hours to do its job of turning that liquid into poop. Sometimes it works faster than that, though it can also take quite a bit longer. This may seem like ages but your colon has a big job to do to create poop from your food. Now all that's left to do is get rid of it...

The Grand Finale

Your sandwich has completed its journey and now we're heading back to the colon—the place where it officially becomes poop and the final part of this wild ride.

When the poop is ready, your colon pushes it into the last section of your large intestine, called the rectum. This is a wide passage about as long as a pencil. Normally, it's empty, but when the poop arrives, it fills up and stretches. This sends a signal to your brain that you need to go to the bathroom... and fast! That's the powerful urge you feel to go.

The moment your brain tells your body to release the poop, your rectum starts to squeeze the poop along. At the same time, the muscles around your anus, the opening where poop finally leaves your body, relax to allow the poop through. It slides out—job done! However, for people with digestive or health issues, this process might be different. They might require a surgical procedure called a colostomy, where waste is removed through a bag before it reaches the rectum and anus.

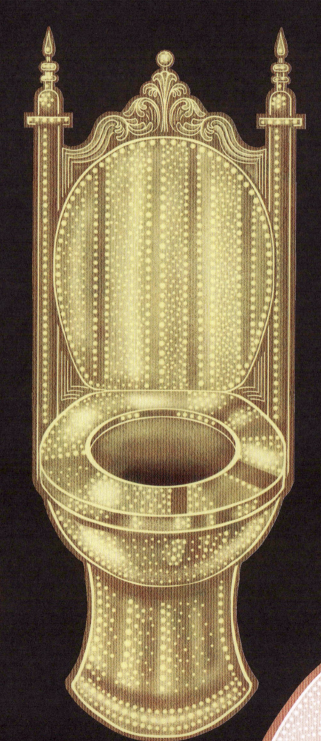

MOST ADULTS PRODUCE 3.5—9 OUNCES OF POOP A DAY. IF YOU STORED ALL YOUR POOP FOR A YEAR, THE STINKY PILE WOULD PROBABLY WEIGH MORE THAN YOU DO! THIS IS NOT RECOMMENDED.

Sit or Squat

Sitting down on a toilet to poop is just one way of doing it. In many cultures around the world, people prefer to squat, getting as close to the floor as possible over a drainage hole. This position is believed to make it easier for the body to eliminate waste without straining.

If you've ever peeked into the toilet before flushing, you might have noticed that fresh poop is shiny. This shine is caused by **mucus** on the surface of the poop. Mucus is a type of slimy substance that covers the insides of your colon and rectum to help the poop slide through. Mucus sticks to poop, making it look shiny, but when poop dries out, this shine disappears.

Before reading this book, you may have thought that going poop was the *most boring thing ever*. A complete waste of time. But now that you know the amazing things your body has done to create that poop, have you changed your mind?

The Truth About Pees, Farts, and Burps

Hang on a minute... we've forgotten something on our incredible journey through the digestive system. We need to look at pee, farts, and burps!

Wonderful pee

Your kidneys—two bean-shaped organs* located near the back of your torso, just below your ribs—are responsible for producing this yellow liquid. They work in a pretty amazing way, filtering out unwanted substances from your blood, along with any excess water and salt, to create wee. The urine then fills up your bladder, which acts like a storage bag. When the bladder is full, muscles at one end relax to let the wee out. The yellow colour of wee comes from a chemical called urobilin (ur–oh–bil–in).

Even though wee may seem like a waste product, it's far from useless. Throughout history, people have used urine for all sorts of things. For example, the Romans used it as a cleaning agent and even put out collection pots for passers-by to pee in (which we definitely wouldn't do today!).

*Most people have two kidneys, though you can live with just one.

Fabulous farts

Farts can be hilarious or gross, depending who you ask. But regardless, they're a *completely normal* bodily function. Farting is simply the release of gas that has built up in your digestive system. Or rather, it's a *mixture* of gases, some of which come from air you swallow and the rest from the friendly bacteria living in your colon, as they digest food (see pages 14–15). So, farting is actually a good thing—it means you're getting rid of those gases. Farting is only a problem if you do it a lot, and this might mean that your digestive system isn't working properly.

Ingredients for a fart:
- Carbon dioxide
- Hydrogen
- Nitrogen
- Methane (optional)
- Hydrogen sulfide—the smelly part

Mix these gases well before serving. Repeat seven or eight times a day!

DID YOU KNOW THERE WAS A FRENCH ENTERTAINER WHO COULD MAKE MUSIC WITH HIS FARTS? HIS NAME WAS JOSEPH PUJOL, AND HE DISCOVERED THAT HE COULD LOUDLY FART A TUNE. HE CALLED HIMSELF "THE FARTER" AND IN THE 1890S AND EARLY 1900S, HIS SPECTACULAR FARTING STAGE SHOW MADE HIM ONE OF THE BIGGEST STARS IN FRANCE.

Belching burps

Before you turn the page, can we have a word about burps? Burps are caused by air that gets trapped in the upper part of your digestive system every time you breathe or swallow. This air ends up in your stomach, and if you don't burp it out, your stomach can become uncomfortably inflated. So, burping is a natural way to release the trapped air and prevent discomfort.

Poop and Health

Everyone poops. Even presidents and prime ministers, royalty, sports stars, celebrities, and your teachers. There's no getting away from it: Poop happens! But did you know that it reveals a lot about your health?

For example, you can tell if you're eating the right kinds of foods just by looking at your poop. So, it's worth keeping an eye out for changes in your poop. No touching, of course, as poop is full of bacteria and other gross things, as we'll find out shortly.

Poop can make us very sick, and amazingly, it can also make us better. Scientists are currently doing lots of exciting research in this field—and some of the things they're discovering are mind-blowing!

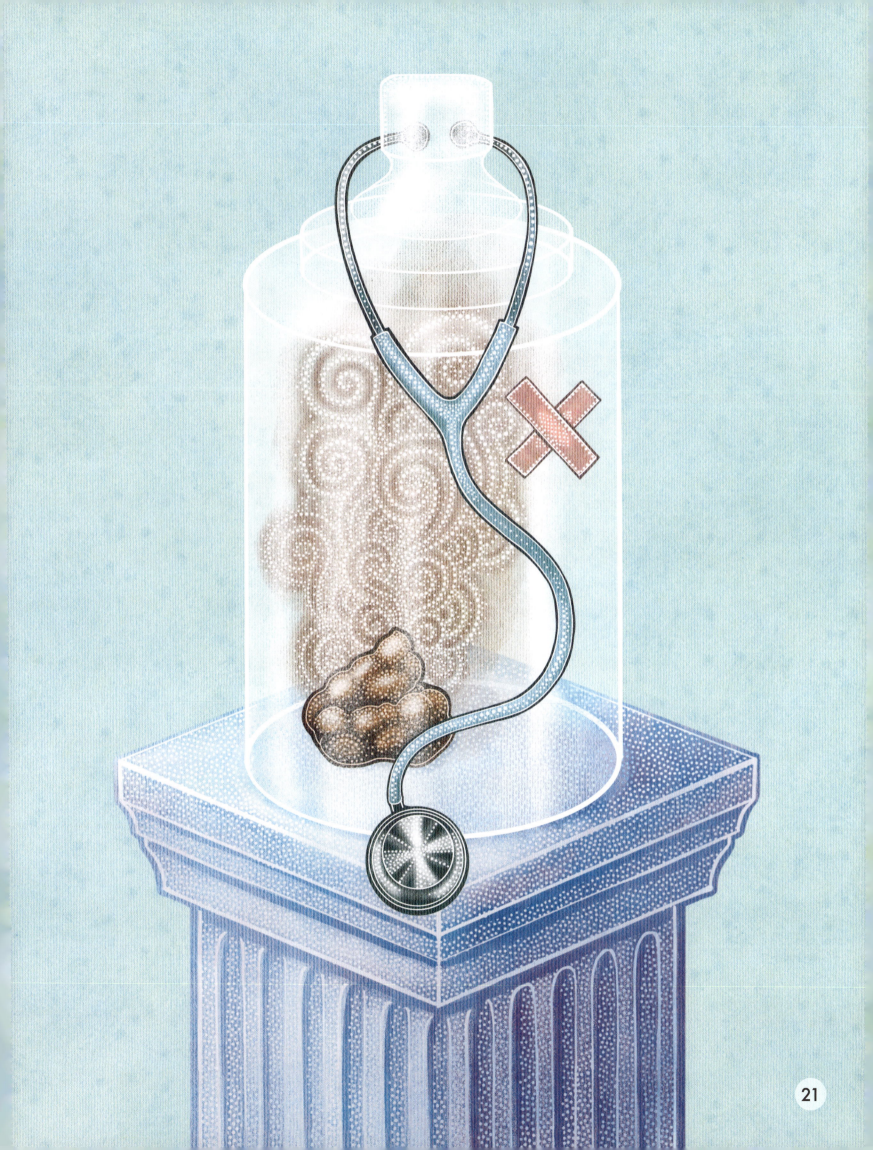

It Takes Guts

Your digestive system does more than just make poop! It's like a bustling world full of billions of microscopic things that live there and play a big part in the health of your gut, which is made up of the small and large intestines in your digestive system. Your gut's main task is to digest food and ultimately produce poop. However, this is not the only job it does...

The gut microbiome

To get a better idea of what it's like inside your gut, imagine you are visiting a rainforest. Inside, there are millions of microbes—like bacteria, fungi, and viruses. Together, they make a big and busy gut community known as your gut microbiome. Your gut microbiome is incredibly important because it has superpowers!

Scientists have discovered that the microbes living in your gut microbiome work together to change what goes on in other parts of your body. For example, your gut can control the sugar levels in your blood, fight off sickness, and even change your mood and mental health!

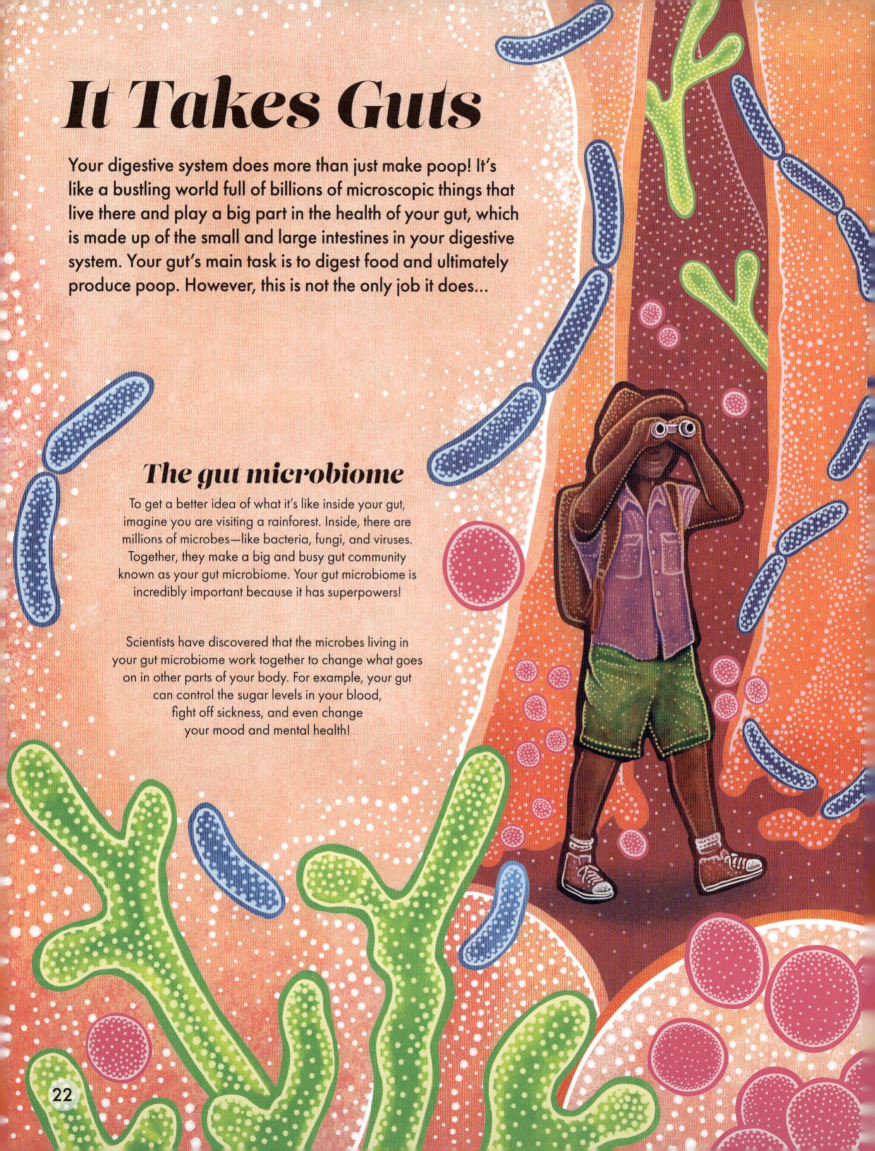

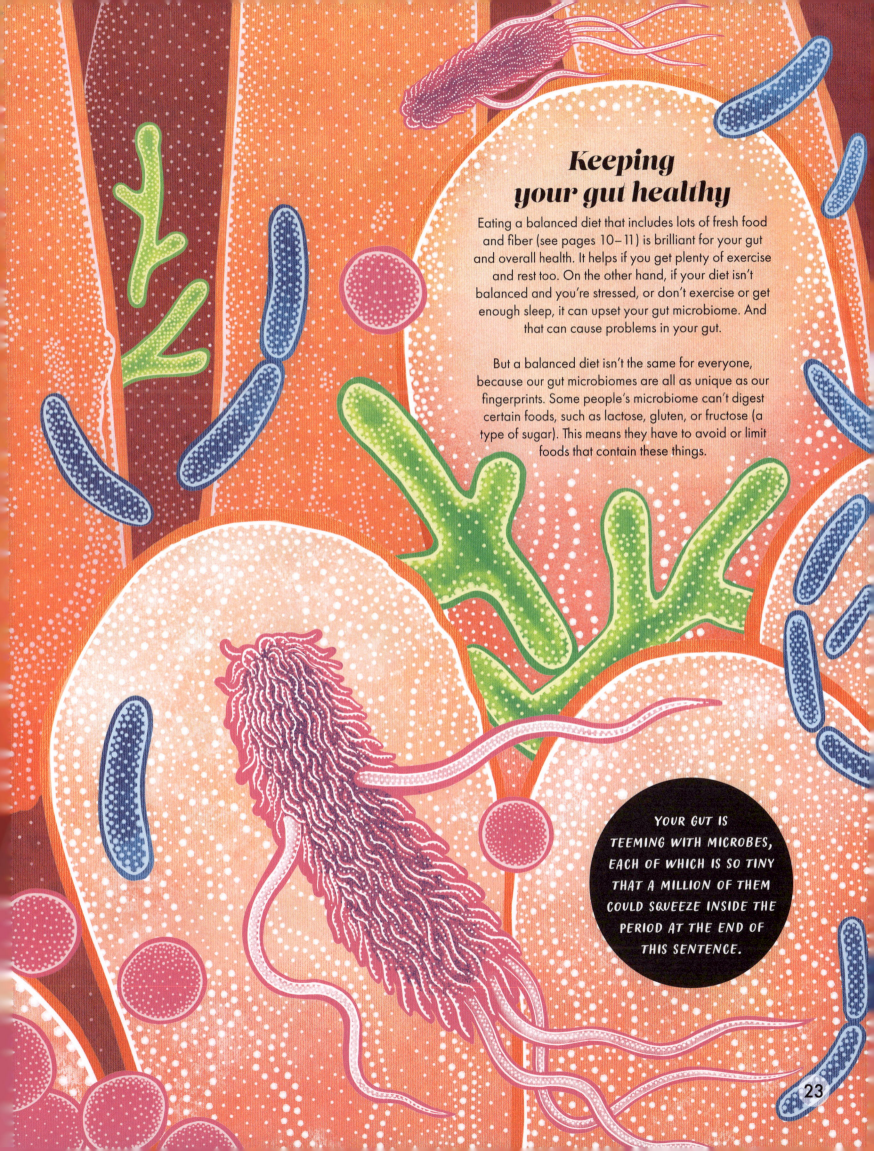

Keeping your gut healthy

Eating a balanced diet that includes lots of fresh food and fiber (see pages 10–11) is brilliant for your gut and overall health. It helps if you get plenty of exercise and rest too. On the other hand, if your diet isn't balanced and you're stressed, or don't exercise or get enough sleep, it can upset your gut microbiome. And that can cause problems in your gut.

But a balanced diet isn't the same for everyone, because our gut microbiomes are all as unique as our fingerprints. Some people's microbiome can't digest certain foods, such as lactose, gluten, or fructose (a type of sugar). This means they have to avoid or limit foods that contain these things.

YOUR GUT IS TEEMING WITH MICROBES, EACH OF WHICH IS SO TINY THAT A MILLION OF THEM COULD SQUEEZE INSIDE THE PERIOD AT THE END OF THIS SENTENCE.

Time to Come Clean

Microscopic germs are present everywhere, and they come in various forms such as bacteria, viruses, fungi, or parasites. They are often harmful and can make us sick. They live in and on our bodies, and our poop is full of them.*

Guarding against germs

This is why, each time you poop, you should *always* wash your hands properly afterward, so these microorganisms go spiralling down the drain.

If you *don't* wash your hands, millions of poop germs will stay on your skin. Then, when you touch other objects, like door handles, light switches, or remote controls, you spread those germs to everything and everyone you touch. When someone else touches those same objects, they will get *your* poop germs on *their* hands and continue spreading them.

* GERMS ARE ALSO FOUND IN SNOT AND IN THE WATER DROPLETS THAT FLY OUT OF OUR MOUTHS WHEN WE COUGH.

Sneaky spreaders

These microbes have one mission: to get inside our bodies. They can sneak in through our mouths and eyes or when we eat something contaminated. And when they get inside us, it's no joke. They can make us feel very sick with food poisoning or diarrhea (die–uh–ree–uh). In some cases, they can even cause infections or diseases.

The nastiest offenders

The worst diseases caused by poop germs include dysentery, cholera, and typhoid. Thankfully, these terrible diseases are now rare in many parts of the world— and there are excellent medicines to help people recover from them. But sadly, many people do still die from these diseases in places where there are not enough toilets, clean, water or soap.

How to wash your hands (properly)

1. Turn on the tap and wet your hands.
2. Apply soap to your hands and rub them together to form a lather.
3. Clean all areas of your hands, including the backs, between your fingers and under your nails. It's recommended that you wash your hands for at least twenty seconds. That's the "Happy Birthday" song, sung twice!
4. Rinse your hands thoroughly and dry them.

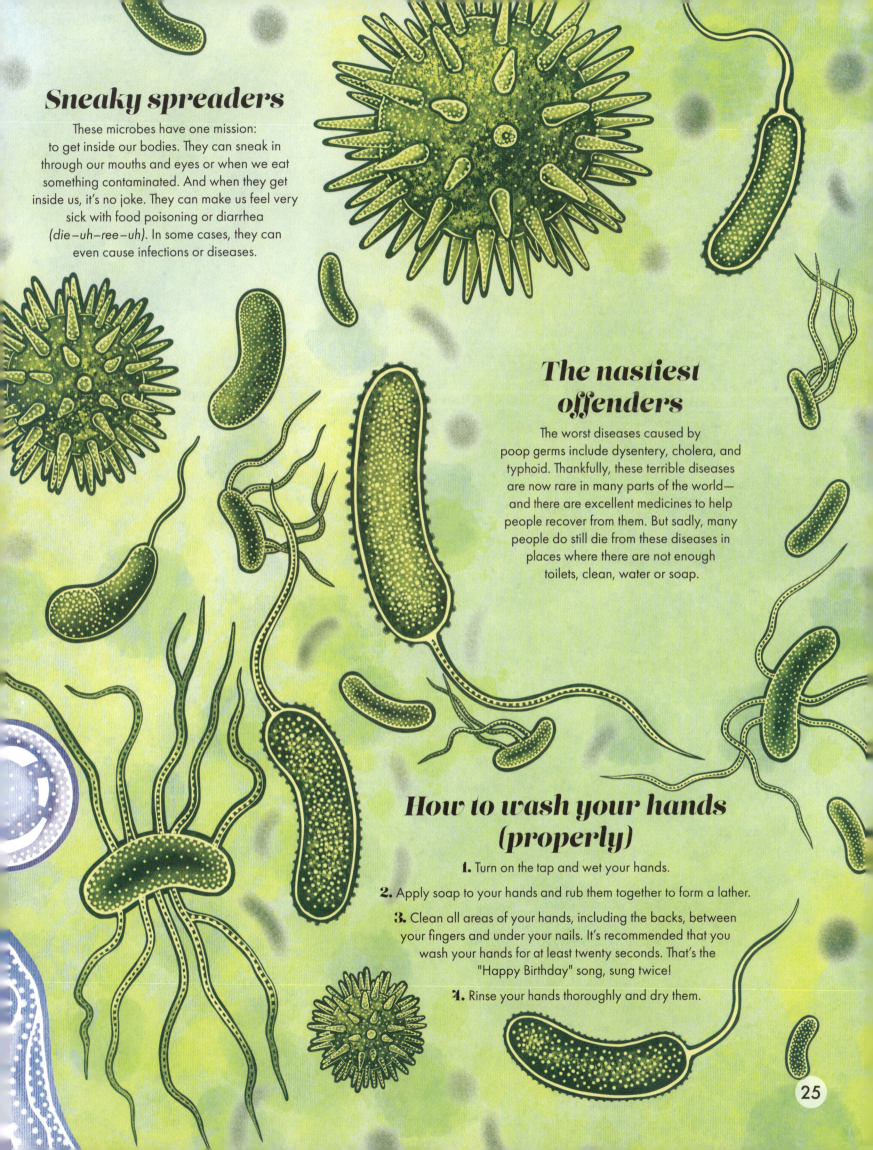

25

Poop Pitfalls

Human poop varies greatly in size, shape, and texture. Don't worry—this is perfectly normal! But ideally, what should it look like?

Doctors and nurses rate a poop's appearance using a special scale called the Bristol Stool Scale. This scoring system was invented in Bristol, England, and "stool" is the medical term for poop. People usually produce Type 3 and 4, which are considered the healthiest and easiest to pass.

The Bristol Stool Scale

TYPE 1
Separate hard lumps, like nuts.

TYPE 2
Lumpy sausage, like a bunch of grapes.

TYPE 3
Sausage with cracks all over it, like a corn on the cob.

TYPE 4
Smooth and soft, like a hot-dog.

TYPE 5
Soft blobs with obvious edges, like chicken nuggets.

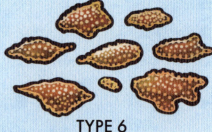

TYPE 6
Fluffy pieces with ragged edges, like oatmeal.

TYPE 7
Liquid, like gravy or brown sauce.

Toilet talk

The best sign that your digestive system is working well is that you visit the toilet regularly.* But wait, what's regular? Well, going between three times a day and three times a week, is the golden range. If this sounds like you, there's nothing to worry about!

* By the way, doctors call going poop a "bowel movement."

What do I do if my poop...

...is an odd color

Sometimes, your poop changes color because of what you eat—not like wild purple with orange spots though! Eating tomatoes, cranberries, and beets can turn it red, while green vegetables can turn it green. Even brightly colored drinks and like ice pops can add a splash of color to your poop. All this is totally normal. But if your poop is yellow, black, or has blood in it, it's time to talk to a trusted adult and visit the doctor.

...seems stuck inside me

From time to time, you may poop less often and it may be hard work. If your poop is dry, hard, and lumpy, it's likely constipation (*kon–stuh–pay–shun*). It can be caused by not eating enough fiber-rich foods. Want to fix it? Eat different foods, drink more water, and be a bit more active. Small changes can get you back to normal!

...is runny

If your poop becomes sloppy, this is called diarrhea. Usually, it's caused by a stomach bug or infection, or eating something disagreeable. Rest at home, drink lots of water, and you're likely to feel better soon. If the problem hasn't gone away after seven days, talk to an adult and see a doctor. You might have a **food intolerance**, which the doctor can advise you about.

> SOME PEOPLE EXPERIENCE A CONDITION CALLED CACOSMIA, WHICH MAKES EVERYTHING SMELL BAD. EVEN PLEASANT THINGS, LIKE ICE CREAM, CAN SMELL LIKE POOP TO THEM. CAN YOU IMAGINE HOW UNPLEASANT THAT WOULD BE?

Poop Potions

Of course, the thought of eating poop or turning it into a drink is revolting and a TERRIBLE IDEA. But in the past, people did just that in an attempt to cure their illnesses.

Poop prescriptions

In ancient Egypt, doctors would prescribe their patients with various types of animal poop—from doggy dung to fly feces. Even crocodile dung was on the menu! The Romans were also at it. They mixed poop with leaves, honey, or wine, before tucking in. These bizarre mixtures were believed to cure everything from flu to snake bites. And in ancient China, people drank "Pu-erh" tea, which was made from dried caterpillar poop. The poop tea was thought to be good for dealing with stomach upsets.

Did these poop cures actually work? Er, well, most of the time, probably not. Sadly, the people who tried these peculiar remedies may have ended up feeling a *whole lot* worse.

CHINA WAS ONE OF THE FIRST PLACES TO USE HUMAN POOP AS MEDICINE, ABOUT 1,700 YEARS AGO. THE POOP WAS BLENDED INTO A TYPE OF SOUP OR JUICE BEFORE DRINKING IT.

Poop power

Today, we know for sure that human poop *can* work as a medicine. Yes, you read that right—scientists have discovered that human poop can help us recover from stomach bugs and infections. (But this does not mean you should start sampling poop any time soon.)

So, here's the scoop on this amazing process...

1) Healthy people who have willingly agreed to be a "poop donor" provide the poop. The donated poop is then tested and treated to ensure it's safe to use.

2) The poop is blended into a milkshake consistency and given to the patient—either through a tube or in a small capsule that is swallowed.

3) Now for the clever part! The friendly bacteria in the donated poop make their way through the patient's digestive system, getting it working properly again!

Scientists have found that this unique human poop medicine can treat various other health issues as well, leading to a *huge* demand for more poop donations. The poop is frozen and stored in "poo banks," ready to be defrosted and used. This is definitely a job for the specialists!

29

The Stuff of Life

How do we know that a rabbit is alive but a rock is not? This may seem an easy question, but it's actually quite complicated. Scientists have identified seven signs of life, and all living things must be able to do *all seven*. Can you think what one of the signs might be? Here's a hint... it's related to excretion,* or getting rid of waste products. Yes, I'm talking about poop.

But hold on, poop is so much more than a waste product. For some animals, it can be a source of food, a place to grow up, a way to communicate, or even a means of defense. In fact, poop is so useful that animals will fight over it.

* The six other signs of life are: movement, nutrition (feeding), respiration (breaking down food for energy), growth, sensitivity (responding to the environment), and reproduction.

Calls of Nature

Animal poop is *fabulous stuff*. But it's not all the same. In fact, many animals leave behind such unique droppings you can easily figure out who the culprit is!

The look and feel of an animal's poop depend on its diet and digestion process. For carnivores like cats and dogs, the process is relatively quick, usually taking less than a day. However, herbivorous mammals like cows take much longer to digest their food due to the tough fiber in plants, which takes several days to process.

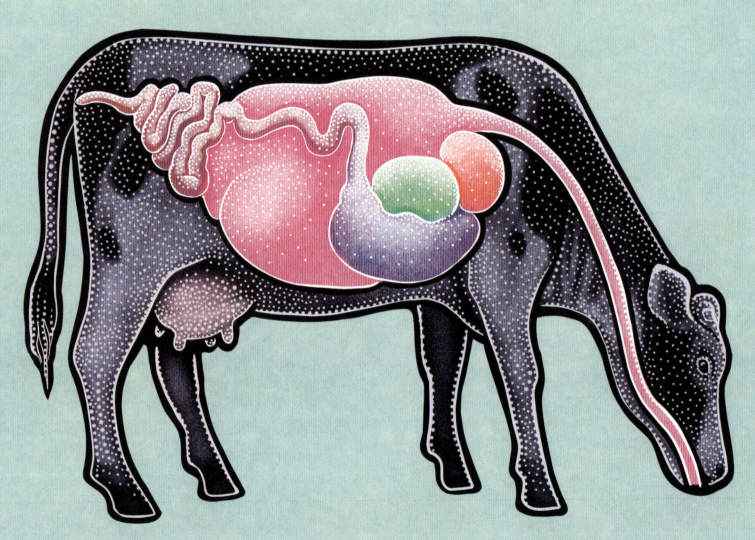

Incredible cow stomachs

Plant-eating animals have evolved special digestive systems to handle the fiber in their food. Cows, for instance, have a massive stomach that is split into four parts, or chambers. This stupendous stomach helps the cows process the colossal amount of grass they eat. They've become so good at breaking down the fiber in grass, their poop squirts out as a slurry that forms a cow pat when it slaps the ground.

Mixing it up

Cows also produce urine, just like we do. And that's because nearly all mammals pee and poop. But this is actually quite unusual! Most other animals, from chickens to crocodiles, don't wee and poop separately. They mix their waste together and then get rid of it at the some time. If you look at a lovely fresh bird poop, the dark bits are "poo" and the white parts are "pee."

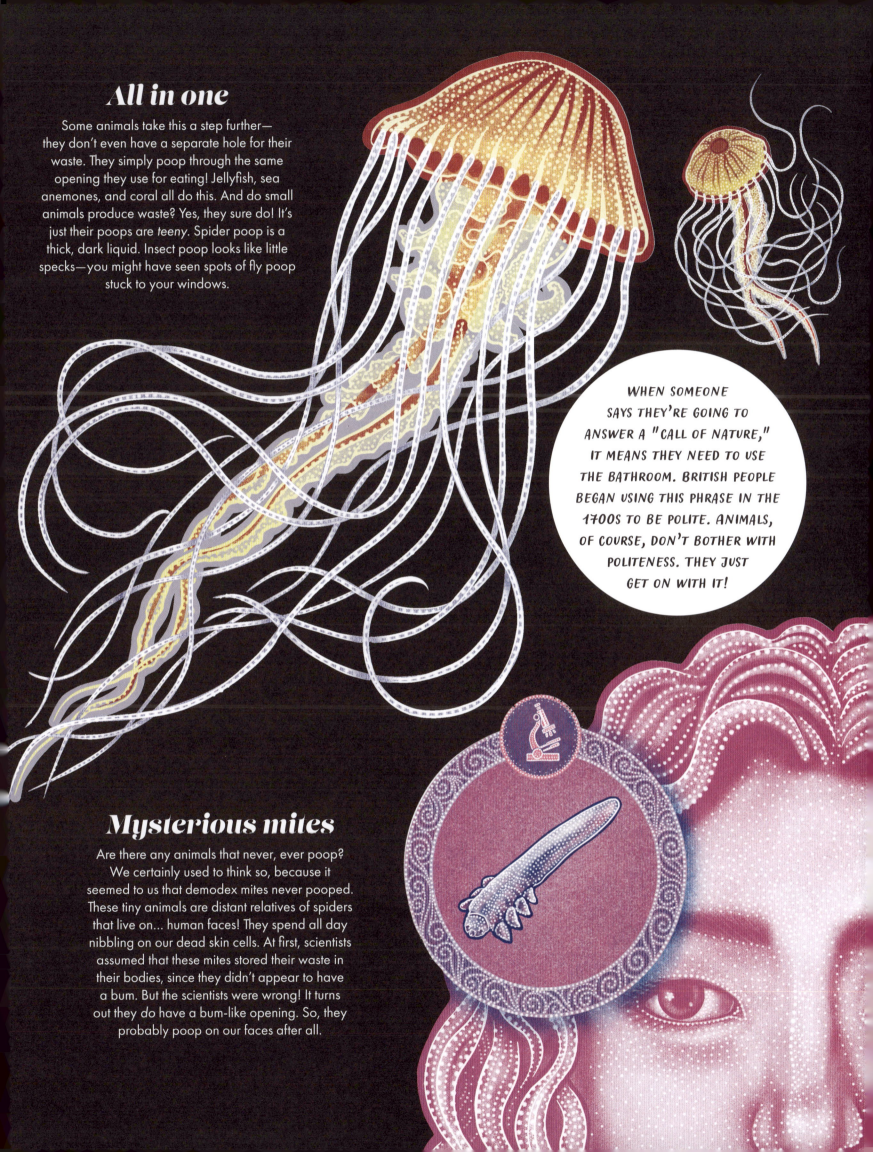

All in one

Some animals take this a step further—they don't even have a separate hole for their waste. They simply poop through the same opening they use for eating! Jellyfish, sea anemones, and coral all do this. And do small animals produce waste? Yes, they sure do! It's just their poops are *teeny*. Spider poop is a thick, dark liquid. Insect poop looks like little specks—you might have seen spots of fly poop stuck to your windows.

WHEN SOMEONE SAYS THEY'RE GOING TO ANSWER A "CALL OF NATURE," IT MEANS THEY NEED TO USE THE BATHROOM. BRITISH PEOPLE BEGAN USING THIS PHRASE IN THE 1700S TO BE POLITE. ANIMALS, OF COURSE, DON'T BOTHER WITH POLITENESS. THEY JUST GET ON WITH IT!

Mysterious mites

Are there any animals that never, ever poop? We certainly used to think so, because it seemed to us that demodex mites never pooped. These tiny animals are distant relatives of spiders that live on... human faces! They spend all day nibbling on our dead skin cells. At first, scientists assumed that these mites stored their waste in their bodies, since they didn't appear to have a bum. But the scientists were wrong! It turns out they do have a bum-like opening. So, they probably poop on our faces after all.

Poop Parade

When it comes to pooping, some animals have a strict routine, while others just go with the flow.

Plenty of animals don't waste any time when it comes to relieving themselves. Birds, for instance, have no qualms about letting it rip while perched or soaring through the skies, day or night. You might have learned this the hard way! Fish and insects are also pros at doing their business on the go. Grazing animals like cows and sheep, with their hefty diets, churn out heaps of dung without hesitation.

On the flip side, many animals are quite selective about where and when they drop their load. Some meticulously distribute their droppings along the borders of their territory, creating a smelly "Keep out!" zone for other animals. However, this display can also attract predators, so some opt to hide it instead.

There's another reason why animals may choose to clean up after themselves. Nasty parasites thrive in feces and can carry diseases. So, keeping their area tidy reduces the risk of illness. horses, for example, always drop their dung in the same corner of their field. Ants even have separate bathroom areas in their nests! Meanwhile, birds use several tricks to keep their nests spick and span. Baby birds package their waste into little "fecal sacs," similar to diapers, for their parents to dispose of. Or they aim their rear end over the edge of their nest to squirt a jet of poop high into the air. It's incredible how far they can fling it!

But does this mean birds never get messy? Not quite! Some birds actually aim to soil their own legs in hot weather to cool down. Penguins are notorious for their messy habits. The sheer amount of waste produced in their crowded colonies even alters the color of the rock or ice. The emperor penguin colonies in Antarctica can be seen from space due to the brown smudges of waste on the ice, which scientists use to identify hidden colonies they never even knew existed.

MOST MAMMALS POOP IN UNDER 20 SECONDS, NO MATTER THEIR SIZE.

Penguins relieve themselves hourly, but what about other animals? Giant pandas go up to forty times a day, while three-toed sloths manage just once a week. Despite having the perfect treetop toilets, sloths slowly climb down to the ground to handle their business before climbing back up again! When they're on the forest floor, moths living in their fur lay eggs in the fresh dung!

35

The Surprising Feast in the Animal Kingdom

For us humans, the idea of dining on poop is gross and definitely unsafe. However, in the animal kingdom, it's a different story. Poop can actually be a valuable source of nutrients.

When animals consume food, their bodies can't extract all the nutrients, so some end up in their waste. This makes poop a tasty dinner for many other creatures. We even have a term for this behavior—coprophagy (kop–row–fah–jee).

Poop connoisseurs

Some animals exclusively dine on poop! Various insects rely on feces for food, including dung beetles, who get their name from how much they *love* the stuff. These beetles prefer their poop fresh and pungent. The stronger the odor, the easier it is for them to find. Dung beetles flock from far and wide to join the feast. They push and shove to claim their share.

Some dung beetles shape the poop into balls, which they roll away. They then bury the dung balls and lay their eggs in them. Later, the wriggly larvae hatch in underground nurseries surrounded by their favorite food—poop!

Most dung beetles go wild for the droppings of large plant-munchers such as cattle, buffalo, antelopes, and elephants. These animals don't fully digest their food, leaving behind a wealth of nutrients for the dung beetles and their larvae to enjoy.

HORNED DUNG BEETLES CAN ROLL POOP BALLS 1,141 TIMES HEAVIER THAN THEIR OWN WEIGHT! THEY ARE SOME OF THE STRONGEST INSECTS ON EARTH.

Stinky snacks

Ever caught a dog munching on poop—maybe even their own? Seems repulsive, doesn't it? But dogs know exactly what they're doing! Poop is full of bacteria, so by eating it, they top up the bacteria in their digestive system, which helps them break down food easier. Baby giant pandas eat their mother's poop because it contains special bacteria that will aid in the digestion of bamboo, which is essential when they start eating their first proper meals.

Nutrient recycling

Rabbits and guinea pigs also tuck into their own poop. In fact, they produce two kinds of poop—one is hard, like mini chocolate balls, and the other is mushy and green. They leave the hard droppings behind, but chomp the soft ones, often directly from their bottom as they pop out! The rabbits digest these special sloppy poops, giving them a second chance to get as many nutrients as they can from their food.

Too Good to Waste

Nothing is wasted in the natural world—and that goes for waste itself! Animals do so many clever things with poop.

Dung detectives

Imagine you're in South Africa, and a white rhino crosses your path. It stops at a huge heap of dung, adds its own contribution, then takes a nice, long sniff. What's going on here? Amazingly, rhinos use these dung heaps to exchange secret messages! Each rhino's dung has a distinct smell, and by sniffing these piles, they can gather information about other rhinos in the area. It's like a social network for rhinos to share status updates!

Stinky camouflage

The larvae of tortoise beetles are protected by armor. But it's not just any armor—it's poop armor! The larvae collect their own poop and mix it with old bits of skin that they have shed from their body. They carry this repulsive shield on their back to fend off enemies.

Whiffy tactics

Hoopoes are colourful birds with spiky crests that do something really sneaky with their poo. Nesting in tree holes, they let their nests fill up with their disgusting droppings, creating a foul smell that keeps predators away. And if that's not enough, their chicks have a defence mechanism too – they can squirt liquid poo at their attackers!

Eau de toilette

Australian birds called rainbow pittas seek out the smelliest poop around to keep their nests safe. Usually, they choose wallaby poop, which has a strong odor that camouflages their own scent, making it hard for tree snakes to locate their nests.

Dung disguise

Some caterpillars look just like bird droppings, complete with lumps, dribble, marks and white splatter. This clever disguise helps them avoid getting eaten by hungry birds, allowing them to move around freely and undisturbed.

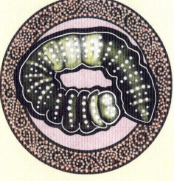

MANY ANIMALS USE URINE TO COMMUNICATE WITH EACH OTHER, TOO. THIS EXPLAINS WHY CATS AND DOGS ARE SO INTERESTED IN SNIFFING AREAS WHERE OTHER ANIMALS HAVE URINATED. THEY ARE ESSENTIALLY CATCHING UP ON ALL THE LOCAL ANIMAL GOSSIP!

Emergency evacuation

When pygmy sperm whales are pursued by orcas, they deploy a remarkable escape strategy. They release a massive cloud of feces, which spreads through the water like a smokescreen, allowing them to escape. Marine biologists and divers nickname these "poonados!"

Poop Through the Ages

Now that we have marveled at how animals poop, let's dive into the fascinating world of human toilet adventures and how humans answer nature's call. As it happens, we also have lots of different ways of going to the bathroom!

Humans built the first toilets as far back as 5,000 years ago. Today, there are both squat and sit-down versions, and in many parts of the world, you will also find various types of drop toilet—a simple seat over a hole in the ground. Plumbing systems? They're like an intricate puzzle, each unique to different countries, just like the distinct customs surrounding the management of our waste.

Over the years, we've dreamed up some ingenious uses for poop. We've even used it to make gunpowder, clothes, and art. When it comes to poop, it seems there's no limit to what we can do with it!

Bathroom Breaks:
From Early Humans' Habits to Ancient Roman Comfort

Toilets have come a long way since they were invented. Here's a brief history of loos from ancient to medieval times.

TOILET PAPER FIRST WENT ON SALE IN 1857. BEFORE THAT, PEOPLE AROUND THE WORLD WIPED WITH ALL SORTS OF STUFF, INCLUDING RAGS, WOOL, SPONGES, LEAVES, MOSS, HAY, AND—AS PAINFUL AS IT SOUNDS!—SEA SHELLS. OR PEOPLE SIMPLY CLEANED THEMSELVES WITH WATER, AS MILLIONS OF US STILL DO TODAY.

2500 BCE
Around 4,500 years ago, the Sumerian people in the Middle East had sit-down toilets in their palaces that looked like brick chairs placed above shallow pits.

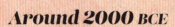

Around 2000 BCE
The Minoan people on the island of Crete in the Mediterranean had stone toilets with wooden seats that actually flushed! They used underground pipes to bring fresh water to the toilets and take the waste away. Similarly, the ancient Egyptians and the Indus Valley Civilization (in today's India and Pakistan) also had advanced toilets around this time.

300,000 years ago

The very first humans lived outdoors and must have relieved themselves outdoors too. We don't know if early humans liked to do their business in a particular place, such as under a tree or among bushes. It could be that they simply "went" wherever they happened to be!

3100–2500 BCE

The oldest indoor toilets, around 5,000 years old, were found in Skara Brae, a Stone Age village on the Scottish island of Orkney. Each little stone house had its own toilet cubicle with a neat hole in the floor for waste. It must have been very chilly in the winter...

221 BCE–207 BCE

An elegant stone toilet was found in the ruins of a palace that belonged to China's Qin Dynasty. It was likely only used by the emperor, his family, and their top officials. Lucky them. The toilet didn't flush, so it had to be manually cleaned by servants. Not so lucky...

43

200 BCE–300 CE

During Roman times, toilets reached new levels of comfort. Public toilets featuring stone or marble benches with rows of holes were constructed throughout the empire. People would chat while using them, and then wipe themselves with a tersorium—a sponge on a stick. Historians think that everyone carried their own, which isn't surprising really. Would you want to share?

1100s–1300s

Within Europe's medieval castles, facilities known as garderobes served as toilets. But these weren't as luxurious as they sound! Essentially, they were just a stone seat on top of a remarkably long chute, where waste would plummet directly into the castle's moat or on to the ground below. The castle's outside walls must have been splattered in excrement and probably stank...

Meanwhile in Africa, remnants of wonderful old toilets have been found in a deserted town near Gedi in Kenya. The abandonment of this once-prosperous African town remains a mystery. But we do know that the inhabitants were skilled engineers as well as traders, because they built stone public toilets that flushed. Their town also had wells where people could fetch clean drinking water.

1300s–1400s

Large portions of present-day Mexico were once ruled by the Aztecs, who knew a thing or two about toilets. They built an amazing city called Tenochtitlan, situated on artificial islands within a lake, creating the illusion of a floating city. The city featured numerous public toilets, which were emptied into... canoes! The poop canoes were then paddled away so that the waste could be spread on fields as fertilizer.

THE ROMANS HAD A GODDESS OF TOILETS, CLOACINA, AND A GOD OF POOP, STERCULIUS.

200-900 CE

The Maya created fabulous stone cities in an area called the Yucatan, encompassing present-day Mexico, Guatemala, and Belize. They engineered sophisticated systems of pipes and canals to supply their cities with fresh water. And they also built impressive lavatories. Thanks to their expertise in high-pressure water systems, their stone toilets flushed beautifully.

1400s-1600s

Over time, wealthy people in Europe wanted their loos to be a little more comfortable and convenient, leading to the adoption of "close stools." These portable stools or boxes, featuring a seat and bowl concealed by a lid, provided a more refined lavatory experience.

As for the ordinary folk, they resorted to simple outdoor shacks to do a number one or two. Or they squatted over a chamber pot—a container kept in their bedroom. Emptying chamber pots into a nearby ditch or trash dump was a daily chore for most people. It was a mucky job and nobody's idea of fun...

Flush With Success

Flushing toilets are one of the most ground-breaking inventions ever. Take a seat and embark on a journey through their history... you might be surprised by what you discover...

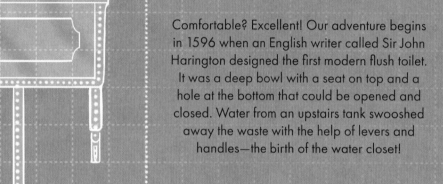

Comfortable? Excellent! Our adventure begins in 1596 when an English writer called Sir John Harington designed the first modern flush toilet. It was a deep bowl with a seat on top and a hole at the bottom that could be opened and closed. Water from an upstairs tank swooshed away the waste with the help of levers and handles—the birth of the water closet!

Many different versions were produced in the years after Harington's brilliant creation. One of them had a clever S-shaped pipe to stop smells from coming up through the drains. It was designed by the Scottish watchmaker Alexander Cumming.

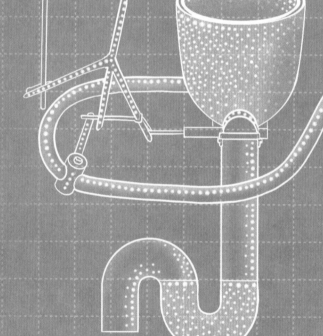

Some of the most famous toilets of all were made in London in Victorian times by the company Thomas Crapper & Co. People often think Crapper invented the toilet, but it's a myth! He did, though, come up with a better flush mechanism that saved lots of water. Of course, the toilets we know and love today use even less water—and they're more comfortable too.

All the buttons

Some of the latest loos have lots of buttons to control their different features. A few of them can even be operated with a remote control or by waving your hand at a sensor. These high-tech toilets offer several types of flushes, warm water, and hot air sprays for cleaning, heated seats, and a self-cleaning system. They're all the rage in Japan and South Korea.

> FLUSHING TOILETS HAVE SAVED COUNTLESS LIVES, AS THEY PREVENT THE SPREAD OF DISEASE. SADLY, OVER 1.5 BILLION PEOPLE WORLDWIDE DON'T HAVE ACCESS TO ONE. IN FACT, MORE PEOPLE HAVE A MOBILE PHONE THAN A PROPER WORKING TOILET.

Squat toilets

Around the world, sitting on a toilet seat is seen as strange. Enter the squat toilet—a low-down ceramic or metal pan at floor level. Users crouch down low over the drainage hole in the middle and a foot pedal triggers the flush. Many people think they're cleaner than sit-down toilets because there's no direct body contact with the surface.

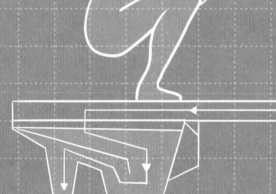

Making Money From Muck

Some people earn a living from dealing in poop. In the past, the brown stuff has even turned a few business owners into millionaires!

Making plants grow

Poop is a fantastic fertilizer, a well-known secret for ages. In the 1800s, as farms in North America and Europe faced the challenge of feeding a booming population, companies started importing seabird poop, known as guano, from islands in the Pacific Ocean. Guano is like rocket fuel for crops, the ultimate fertilizer. Mountains of the snow-white guano had built up on these islands over hundreds of years, until it lay on the ground up to 164 feet deep. Crews worked in terrible conditions to shovel the guano on to waiting ships. Tons of the stuff was then shipped to North America and Europe every year. The owners of the guano trading companies became so rich that people started referring to guano as "white gold."

IN 1864—1866, A CONFLICT KNOWN AS THE GUANO WAR BROKE OUT BETWEEN SPAIN, PERU, AND CHILE. THEY WERE FIGHTING FOR CONTROL OF THE ISLANDS WHERE SEABIRD GUANO CAME FROM.

Working wonders with dog poop

Responsible dog owners today always carefully dispose of their pets' waste. But in the past, people would have been *shocked* by this. In those days, dog poop was valuable... People would search the streets for as much dog poop as they could find and sell it to leather factories, or tanneries. This was a well-paid job, carried out by adults and sometimes even by children. Leatherworkers wanted the dog poop *really* badly because it had an incredible property. When they added the poop to tubs of water and soaked animal skins in it, the skins turned soft and supple, perfect for making beautiful leather. The workers would rub the revolting liquid onto the skins with their bare hands. Don't try this at home.

Going with a bang

For centuries, poop was also a key ingredient in gunpowder. Dung from cattle, pigs, and pigeons was used, and bat droppings from caves were particularly good. Once the dung was old and rotten, like crumbly soil, a chemical called potassium nitrate was extracted. This chemical reeked, but people put up with the awful smell. They then mixed it with other chemicals to produce gunpowder—a black powder that explodes when lit. Gunpowder was made this way until about 175 years ago, when the first poop-free explosives were invented.

The Great Stink

In 1858, the stench of sewage that hung over London grew so bad, something had to be done about it...

By the 1800s, major cities like London had become unbelievably filthy. The system of managing waste and sewage could no longer cope because the number of people living in the cities had grown so quickly.

The task of waste disposal largely fell upon "night soil workers." Under the cover of darkness, they would collect "night soil"—that's poop and pee—from the city's toilets and chamber pots. The workers would then transport the waste for use as fertilizer on fields or simply dump it on muck heaps. But a lot of poop still ended up in the streets or sloshed into the city's drains and streams. From there, it found its way into the River Thames, which flowed through the center of London.

The River Thames stank. Londoners were used to seeing horrible things floating in the murky brown water, but the stench in July and August 1858 was on a whole other level. Hot weather made the nose-wrinkling smell worse and worse, until it was impossible to walk near the polluted river without gagging. The Houses of Parliament, situated on the River Thames, had to keep every window closed. Thousands of people got sick and even died from the contaminated water. It became known as the Great Stink.

That summer, politicians finally voted for a massive building project to solve London's poop problem. Joseph Bazalgette, the city's top engineer, was in charge. His solution? The implementation of an intricate network of drains and sewers (underground pipes and channels for human waste) to be installed beneath the city. This network would not only manage sewage (human waste), but also rainwater. The sewers would carry the waste far from the capital, cleaning up the River Thames.

Workers dug up huge areas of the city to build the many miles of sewers, which were lined with bricks. Several of the sewers were as big as the tunnels later used for underground trains! In 1875, the amazing new sewer system was at last complete. It could carry more than five hundred million gallons of waste every day. The work had cost a colossal amount. In today's money, a project on this scale would cost billions of dollars.

It did the trick, though, and the stink went away. The death rate in the city also went down. Now that there was less poop everywhere, it didn't get into the drinking water, and there was far less sickness. Londoners became much healthier thanks to sewers.

Joseph Bazalgette's sewers have been called one of the wonders of the industrial world and were later copied by cities across the globe.

THE ROMANS CONSTRUCTED A SUPERB NETWORK OF SEWERS IN ANCIENT ROME. THE LARGEST WAS CALLED THE CLOACA MAXIMA. IT STILL SURVIVES, THOUGH IT'S NO LONGER IN USE.

51

A Gift That Keeps on Giving

Poop is all around us and doesn't cost a thing. No wonder people have always been creative with it. But it's best to leave the innovative poop uses to the experts and not experiment yourself!

> DARING FASHION DESIGNERS HAVE CREATED DRESSES OUT OF COW DUNG. THE POOP IS DRIED, THEN TURNED INTO A UNIQUE KIND OF FABRIC. YOU'D NEVER GUESS WHAT THESE FROCKS ARE MADE OF!

Poop-ular event

When dry, cow pats fly really well. And in the U.S., where the discs of dung are called cow pies or cow chips, people chuck them for sport! Every April, the world championship is held in Beaver, Oklahoma. The record throw is just under 189 feet.

Beauty and the bird

In Japan, a cosmetic moisturizer is made from the droppings of a little bird called the Japanese bush warbler. The unusual beauty product was first used as a facial cream hundreds of years ago—and some people still use it. Geishas, who are traditional Japanese performers, once used it to remove their make-up.

Cat-poo-cino

One of the world's most expensive coffees comes from the droppings of an Asian palm civet. This cat-like animal adores the fruit that grows on coffee plants, but its body can't digest the hard beans in the middle of the fruit. So, the undigested beans end up in its poop. Farmers in Indonesia gather the civet poop, pick out the beans, then wash and roast them. Fans of the civet coffee say it tastes *delicious* and they call it "cat-poo-cino." Sadly, farms often mistreat the civets, so the way that this coffee is made is not the only thing that may keep people from drinking it.

Dung deal

Today, most paper is made from a watery soup of tree fiber known as pulp. But many other kinds of natural fiber can be used too... including elephant dung! In Africa and Asia, where elephants are from, the dung is carefully boiled, washed, mixed with straw, bark, or leaves, then pressed into paper. About one hundred ten pounds of elephant dung makes 125 sheets of A4 paper.

Works of art

In 1961, the Italian Piero Manzoni created a very strange artwork—ninety tin cans of his own poop! Some claim that he filled the cans with something else, but we may never know the truth (well, unless someone opens one). Manzoni wasn't the only one at it. British artist Chris Ofili is known for his paintings that use elephant poop alongside other materials.

Going potty

Cow dung can even be turned into pots and plates. The secret is an amazing material called merdacotta— basically dry cow dung, straw, and clay. It was invented in Italy at a museum of poop. (Australia and Japan also have a poop museum. And there's one in England too—on the Isle of Wight.)

Poop Planet

Earth is often called the "Blue Planet" because three-quarters of its surface is covered with water. But maybe we should call our home "Poop Planet" instead. As far as we know, Earth is the only planet where feces exist, and that makes it very unique...

When added to soil, poop helps plants grow strong and healthy. It is also used to build homes, burned to keep people warm, and it can even generate electricity! When used carefully, it's incredible stuff.

But the problem is, by 2030 farm animals and humans will produce a staggering 5.5 billion tons of poop per year.* This immense amount poses a significant challenge. If we just dump it all in rivers, lakes, and seas, it can cause great harm to the environment. So, let's look at the ways we can use it to make the world a better place instead.

*You would need 895,000,000 double-decker buses to transport this!

Poop to the Rescue

While many may find the topic cringe-worthy, poop can help nature to thrive in wonderful ways and shape our planet.

Planet-protecting poop

Whales are the largest animals on Earth—and their poops are colossal. When certain whales poop, the orange or pink stain in the water is so big it can be seen from an aircraft in the sky. This excrement contains an abundance of nutrients that serve as food for tiny plants, known as phytoplankton *(fy–tow–plank–tuhn)*. And just like plants on land, these minuscule plants play a crucial role in Earth's ecosystem. If there's too much carbon dioxide in the atmosphere, it heats up, which is bad news for our planet. But these micro plants actually absorb carbon dioxide, releasing oxygen, which means they're fighting climate change! So every time a whale does its business it is helping Earth stay healthy!

SOME SEEDS WON'T GROW UNLESS AN ANIMAL EATS THEM FIRST AND POOPS THEM OUT. NATURE CAN BE FUNNY SOMETIMES.

Poop-powered forests

Many animals eat delicious fruits, and the seeds end up in their poop. Orangutans, for example, eat figs but cannot digest the seeds, so they pass into the shaggy apes' poop. By chomping and pooping, the orangutans spread the fig seeds across the forest floor. And, as they also eat various fruit from other trees and plants, orangutans spread the other seeds throughout the forest too. They're not the only creatures that do this—animals large and small do the same thing in forests all over the world. Simply by living their lives, these animals are helping our forests grow.

Super worms make super poop

One of the *most amazing* things about earthworms is probably their poop. Earthworm waste is packed with nutrients, providing the soil with the essential elements that plants need to grow. That's not all—these earthworms mix up the soil, creating tiny tunnels and lots of holes that fill with air. This keeps the soil healthy, producing an ideal environment for plant growth. This is why worms are great news for farmers, gardeners, and our planet! Maybe we should call them "superworms" instead!

Building Blocks

What would you use to build a home? Something affordable, strong, and easy to find? Believe it or not, poop fits the bill! Around the world, many homes are made out of this surprising material.

Cozy homes

Humans, too, are brilliant at building with poop. In places like Mexico, South America, Africa, Turkey, and southern Asia, people craft houses using the dung from their cows or donkeys, adhering to age-old practices. In India, it's common to see rural homes plastered with polished, dried cow dung. After drying to eliminate any odor, the dung creates a smooth layer that insulates homes, keeping them warm in winter and cool in summer.

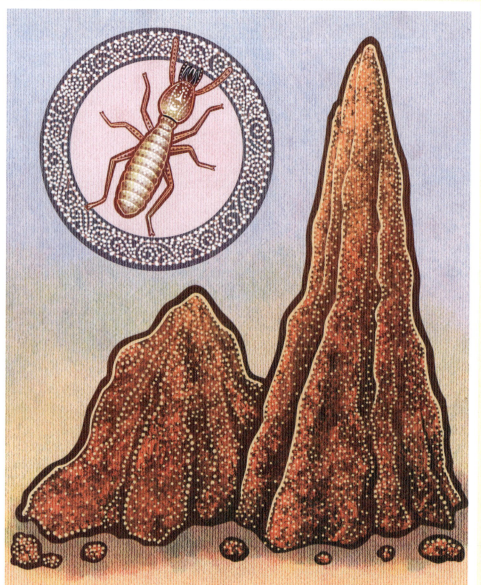

Termite towers

Ant-like insects called termites are experts at making homes out of poop. These clever critters build huge nests using soil, grass, and even their own excrement as a form of glue. Some termite mounds in Africa are taller than giraffes, housing several million termites inside. The termite-poop glue is so strong, the humongous mounds never collapse.

Building with poop

To build a house using poop, the first step is often to make a frame for the walls from planks and sticks. Next, you cover the frame with a paste made from animal dung mixed with straw, mud, and water. Finally, you allow this mucky mixture to dry, which creates a rock-hard surface. Walls built this way can last for hundreds of years.

Eco-friendly construction

People have been building with poop for thousands of years—and some architects say we should be using it even more today. Many conventional building materials, such as concrete, steel, and ordinary bricks, take lots of energy and resources to make, and then they have to be transported around the world to where they are needed. But poop is natural and it's everywhere, so building homes with poop is much better for the environment!

PEOPLE IN WEST AFRICA AND INDIA ADD COLOR TO WET COW DUNG AND USE IT TO PAINT BEAUTIFUL PATTERNS ON THE WALLS AND FLOOR OF THEIR HOMES.

ANOTHER WAY TO BUILD HOUSES WITH POOP IS BY TURNING THE POOP INTO BRICKS. THIS IS BEST LEFT TO THE EXPERTS...

HOW TO MAKE POOP BRICKS

1) Add straw, mud and water to animal dung.
2) Mix it really well.
3) Bake the mixture under the hot sun or in a kiln oven.
4) Cut the hard, dry material into bricks.

Rescuing the River

Poop can become a problem when it contaminates water, as it can be harmful to nature and pose a risk to human health.

There once was a fisherman who had a favorite river. Its crystal-clear water sparkled and was home to herons, kingfishers, and dragonflies. Every week when the man visited, he caught lots of fish. But as the years rolled by, the river began to change.

The water turned sludgy and green, it smelled foul and the fisherman barely caught anything. He even saw dead fish wash up on the riverbank. The herons, kingfishers, and dragonflies were gone, too. What went wrong?

Sadly, the fisherman's beloved river was full of sewage—the human waste from a nearby town. Whenever it rained, the town's aging sewers filled up with rainwater and overflowed, releasing their waste straight into the once-pristine river. And there was something else in the river that thrived on this sewage—plant-like organisms called algae (al–gee). When the algae fed on the sewage, they grew rapidly. Eventually, the algae formed a thick scum on the surface of the river and used up all the oxygen in the water, causing most of the river's plants and animals to die.

It was time to act! The fisherman launched a campaign to prevent sewage from being pumped into the river. Thousands of people joined the campaign. One day, these activists may win their battle, and if they do, the river will recover and its plants, fish, and birds will return.

Not just one river's problem...

Rivers, streams, lakes, and ponds worldwide all face the same problem, becoming clogged with sewage and pollution, killing the wildlife that lives there. Some of the pollution is human waste and some of it comes from farm animals—often chickens, cows, and pigs. Even the ocean isn't safe as poop pollution can ruin coral reefs, which are home to huge numbers of sea creatures.

Sewage treatment plants

Poop pollution is a *huge* problem. But luckily, there's a solution. Modern sewage treatment plants collect wastewater—that's dirty water from toilets, bathrooms, and washing machines—usually through a network of pipes. They remove any solid waste and destroy the harmful bacteria in the water. The clean water can then be safely returned to rivers, lakes, or the ocean. The leftover solid waste is used on farms as fertilizer, burned as fuel, or transformed into biogas (as we will see on the next page).

WHEN WATER IS POLLUTED BY POOP, BACTERIA IN THE WATER SPREAD INCREDIBLY FAST. MANY OF THE BACTERIA CAN DOUBLE THEIR NUMBERS EVERY THIRTY MINUTES!

Risks for us humans

Not only is wildlife threatened by poop pollution, but humans are at risk as well. Drinking, swimming, or bathing in contaminated water can make us sick, as it contains bacteria and viruses.

61

Can Poop Save the World?

Yes, it sure can, because poop can be a superhero! Let's have a look at how...

Food from poop

While consuming poop is, of course, an absolute no-no, we do eat food that's been grown with the help of poop. This isn't something new—humans have been using the stuff to boost their crops for millennia. Animal and human waste contains many essential nutrients that plants need, particularly nitrogen, phosphorus, and potassium. To this day, farmers all over the world still enrich their fields with manure from farm animals, giving plants a nutrient-packed treat.

Energy from poop

Animal dung isn't just good for plants, it's a fantastic fuel too. Back in the day, our resourceful ancestors burned dung for warmth, and even today, people worldwide rely on their animals' dung for fuel. But we also have another clever way to get energy from poop...

Around the world, poop is collected and pumped into sealed tanks called digesters. Inside the tanks, the waste is broken down by microscopic organisms, which release gas. The gas is mostly methane and carbon dioxide, and we call it biogas. Biogas can be used to power vehicles and ships and create electricity for factories or even whole neighborhoods in a city. The great thing about biogas is that it's a clean fuel. Unlike many other kinds of fuel, biogas does not create pollution or cause climate change. This is just another way that poop is contributing to the wellbeing of our planet.

Minerals from poop

Did you know that your body has very tiny bits of gold, silver, and copper in it? And these tiny pieces of metal get into your poop (although there's no need to go hunting for treasure there!). Your poop also contains dozens of other valuable minerals. Admittedly, there are only minuscule amounts of these minerals in each stool.* But there's a way that we can get bigger dollops of minerals from human poop...

Scientists are figuring out how to remove minerals from the poop of entire cities. This is made possible as waste passes through sewage treatment plants! Perhaps, in the future, we could source the materials for gadgets such as cell phones from our own poop, instead of having to dig these minerals out of the ground!

*It would take you hundreds of years to poop enough gold to make a solid gold ring.

A COMPANY HAS INVENTED A PORTABLE MACHINE THAT CONVERTS HUMAN POOP INTO DRINKING WATER. ONE DAY, MACHINES LIKE THIS COULD POTENTIALLY PROVIDE MILLIONS OF PEOPLE WITH ACCESS TO A SAFE AND CLEAN WATER SUPPLY.

The Science of Poop

Almost everyone, young or old, is fascinated by poop. There are even scientists who study poop for a living, and it's amazing what they can learn through their examinations.

Doctors and vets also take a keen interest in poop. They often need to rely on fecal samples to pinpoint the source of infections or to detect signs of disease in their patients. But remember—all these professionals take great care when they handle poop, like wearing gloves and face masks in special laboratories. It's best to leave excrement analysis to the experts.

However, there *is* one poop experiment that is safe for you to try—to find out more, turn the page...

Blue Poop Challenge

Ready for a delicious science experiment? The Blue Poop Challenge is a simple—and tasty—experiment to discover how long it takes for your body to produce poop.

Scientists are always exploring new ways of conducting their research. One team of scientists who study the human digestive system decided to create a safe experiment that's so much fun. The Blue Poop Challenge aims to uncover the journey of food through your body, and surprisingly, it involves baking muffins. If you can bake (or can persuade someone to bake for you!) then this is the challenge for you.

Here's what you need to do:

- Ask an adult to help you make two muffins using bright blue food dye.*

- Eat the muffins for breakfast and make a note of the time and date.

- Whenever you visit the toilet, glance at your poop. When the first blue poop appears, mark down the time and date again.

- Figure out how long the blue food took to travel through your body.

* For full instructions, search online for #bluepoopchallenge

Understanding your results

Most participants find that it takes between **14 hours** and **58 hours** for blue poop to appear.* If your timing falls within this range—fantastic! It means that your gut microbiome is nice and healthy. (We first met the gut microbiome on pages 22–23—it's the community of microbes living in your digestive system.)

If your blue poop appears in less than 14 hours or takes longer than 58 hours, don't worry! This could simply indicate an imbalance in your gut microbiome or a reaction to something you have eaten. When this happens, your body may have difficulties digesting food and producing poop. Poop habits can vary, and the chart on page 26 illustrates the variations in poop appearance. Of course, if you're ever worried about your poop habits or something doesn't feel right, you should speak to a trusted adult and visit a doctor.

Anyone can upload their blue poop findings to the Blue Poop Challenge website. These results give the scientists who created the challenge lots of interesting information about the pooping habits of thousands of people, which is really useful for their research. It's awesome what a few blue muffins can tell us!

* The average time is around 28–29 hours.

Every Poop Tells a Story

Did you know that people have been fascinated by poop for a very long time? We study poop because it can tell us many things.

Poop inspectors

In ancient China, the powerful emperors had dedicated doctors. And their jobs included... studying the emperors' poop. The fresh poop was carefully inspected to see if anything might be wrong with it. Thankfully, modern methods have replaced this unhygienic practice today...

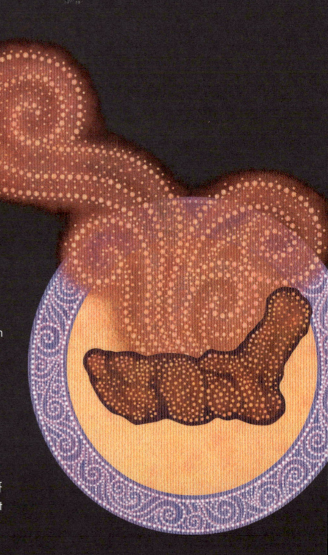

Poop clues

Some ancient poops have turned into fossils (a fossil is anything that remains from an organism that lived long ago). The fossilized poops are like stones and we call them coprolites *(kop–rol–ites)*. They are *incredibly* useful clues for scientists who study dinosaurs. By examining them, scientists can figure out what dinosaurs used to eat. Some dino coprolites have the remains of beetles, leaves, or grass in them. But the coprolites of carnivorous dinosaurs are full of crunched-up bones!

The largest coprolite ever found is a whopping 27 inches long, and was excreted by a T rex. It's so famous that it has actually been given a name ... Barnum!

Poop left behind by humans who lived long ago can also turn into fossils. By studying these relics, we're able to see back in time and learn about the lives of our ancestors. The fossilized poops can tell us what people ate, as well as what infections and diseases people had thousands of years ago.

You are what you poop

Poop has something called DNA in it, which is a material found in the cells of *all* living things. DNA is a complex set of instructions for how to make a body, like the code for a website. Amazingly, the DNA of every single animal on Earth is different. Scientists can study the DNA in waste to figure out which animal it came from. The DNA in the poop is like a signature that tells you who did it!

Imagine you're a scientist studying leopards in Africa. By collecting and analyzing their poop, you can determine the number of leopards living in a given area, their gender, age, and how far each leopard travels every night. This information is invaluable, especially because leopards are shy creatures who often only come out at night, making it difficult to see them. But it's much easier to find their poop. By studying leopard poop, scientists can learn all about these big cats without ever seeing them.

SCIENTISTS HAVE SOME PRETTY COOL WAYS OF COLLECTING ANIMAL EXCREMENT. TO CATCH WHALE POOP, THEY FLY DRONES LOW OVER THE SEA TO SCOOP IT OFF THE SURFACE OF THE WATER!

Space Poop Odyssey

Venturing into space is an extraordinary experience for humans, but even in the cosmos, we still need to answer calls of nature. Unfortunately, it's a bit trickier when you're far above the Earth.

Our bodies are designed for living on Earth, which makes things awkward on space missions. In space, there's no air, so we can't breathe normally. Astronauts experience weightlessness, causing them to float around unless they are secured to something. Which makes you wonder, what do they do when they need to go to the bathroom?

The first space flights

In the early 1960s, space flights only lasted a few hours. To relieve themselves, astronauts peed into socks made of rubber, or they wore giant diapers. Pooping wasn't a problem, because the astronauts went to the bathroom before their rocket blasted off, and they had landed back on Earth before they needed to go again.

Hoses and bags

As space missions extended to multiple days, astronauts used a hose that squirted their urine into space and collected their poop in bags that were attached to their body. After each use, the astronauts sealed the bags and squeezed them to release chemicals that killed bacteria in the poop. They then rolled the bag up and stored it away until their return to Earth.

Poop on the Moon

When American astronauts visited the Moon, they left bags of waste behind. So there are still 96 bags of poop on the Moon! (Though it might now be just dust.) At the time, the astronauts didn't really have a choice—they had to dump the poop to make their spacecraft lighter for the return journey to Earth. On future missions to the Moon, astronauts will probably bring it all home with them.

Space toilets

The first ever space toilet was launched aboard the Russian Soyuz in 1967. Modern space toilets, found on the U.S. Space Shuttles and the International Space Station, use air jets to collect and containers to store solid waste. Toilets on airplanes work in a similar way, except there's one BIG difference in space. Astronauts always hold on tight to their space toilet—or they'll float off!

ASTRONAUTS' POO HAS SOMETIMES "ESCAPED" AND FLOATED THROUGH THE CABIN OF THEIR SPACECRAFT!

Recycling Pee

On the International Space Station, very little is wasted. So the crew's urine is turned into clean water for them to drink and wash with. The same recycling system will be needed on any spaceship that takes humans to Mars. As the epic journey to Mars and back will take almost two years, the spaceship's crew will have to reuse *everything* on board. If humans set up a base on Mars, they might even turn their poop into fertilizer to grow crops there.

Whose Poop?

Animal poop comes in many different shapes, sizes, colors, and textures. It can even be pink or sparkle like glitter! In this guide, you'll see some weird and wonderful animal poop from every corner of the planet.

Warning! DON'T TOUCH! Remember: it's OK to look at animal poop, but *never* ever handle the poop or pick it up. Take a photo of it instead.

STINK-O-METER — 1 NOT STINKY, 2 MODERATELY PUNGENT, 3 POSITIVELY PUTRID

Garden snail
Cornu aspersum

SHAPE: Tiny squiggles left on leaves
COLOR: Dark green
SMELL: 1
COOL FACT: Snails poop through the same hole that they breathe through.

Caterpillars
Lepidoptera

SHAPE: Tiny grains called "frass"
COLOR: Usually black, but can be green or yellow
SMELL: 1
COOL FACT: Some caterpillar poop falling from the treetops sounds like rain.

Brown bear
Ursus arctos

SHAPE: Chunky, often with fur, bones, fish scales, or seeds in it
COLOR: Brown or black, but turns red when bears eat berries
SMELL: 1 (2 if a bear eats meat)
COOL FACT: When bears hibernate for the winter, they don't poop for five to seven months.

Spotted hyena
Crocuta crocuta

SHAPE: Nuggets the size of table-tennis balls
COLOR: Green at first, then turns white
SMELL: 2
COOL FACT: The whiteness of the poop comes from bones that the hyenas crunch up and eat.

Blue whale
Balaenoptera musculus

SHAPE: Like lumpy gravy and forms a giant cloud in the water
COLOR: Pink or orange
SMELL: 3
COOL FACT: Each massive blue whale poop is up to 53 gallons.

Wombat
Vombatus ursinus

SHAPE: Hard cubes, like little loaves of bread
COLOR: Brown
SMELL: 2
COOL FACT: Wombats squeeze their poop into cubes to get goodness out of their food.

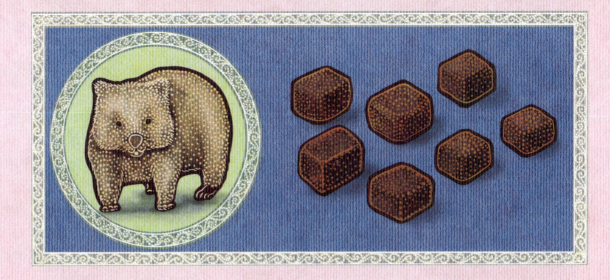

Pine marten
Martes martes

SHAPE: Similar to long, twisted cat poops
COLOR: Black, but turns red or blue when berries are eaten
SMELL: 1
COOL FACT: Pine martens wiggle while pooping, which twists the poop.

European hedgehog
Erinaceus europaeus

SHAPE: Small black tubes, with a pointed end
COLOR: Black and shiny
SMELL: 1
COOL FACT: Hedgehog poop sparkles because it's full of broken bits of insects.

River otter
Lutra lutra

SHAPE: Slimy heaps of poop called "spraints," full of fish bones and scales
COLOR: Black
SMELL: 3
COOL FACT: Otters produce special jelly to help their bony poops slide through their bodies.

Common garter snake
Thamnophis sirtalis

SHAPE: Squishy tubes full of fur and bone
COLOR: Black or brown, with white parts
Smell: 2
COOL FACT: The white parts of snake poop are actually pee.

American bison (buffalo)
Bison bison

SHAPE: Like cow pats. Called "buffalo chips" in North America.
COLOR: Brown or greenish
SMELL: 2
COOL FACT: Some Native American peoples, such as the Sioux and Comanche, used to burn buffalo chips as fuel.

73

African savanna elephant
Loxodonta africana

SHAPE: Mighty dollops of dung, full of plant material such as grass
COLOR: Greenish-yellow when fresh. Brown when dry.
SMELL: 1
COOL FACT: Each load of elephant poop weighs more than a car tire.

Mexican red-knee tarantula
Brachypelma hamorii

SHAPE: Like grains of rice
COLOR: White
SMELL: 1
COOL FACT: Tarantulas are tidy animals that always poop in the same place.

Koala
Phascolarctos cinereus

SHAPE: Little pellets
COLOR: Dark green
SMELL: 1
COOL FACT: Mother koalas release a special creamy poop called "pap" for their babies to eat.

Adélie penguin
Pygoscelis adeliae

SHAPE: Liquid
COLOR: Pink. The color comes from shrimp-like animals that the penguins eat.
SMELL: 2
COOL FACT: Penguins are powerful poopers. They fire their poop more than three feet away from their bottoms.

Red fox
Vulpes vulpes

SHAPE: Squishy sausages, often with fur and bones in it
COLOR: Black, grey, brown, or purplish
SMELL: 3
COOL FACT: Red foxes sometimes eat dog poop, which has plenty of nutrients in it.

Tiger
Panthera tigris

SHAPE: Similar to pet cat poop, but much bigger
COLOR: Black or brown
SMELL: 3
COOL FACT: Tiger poop smells nasty, but reports say their pee smells like buttered popcorn.

Great white shark
Carcharodon carcharias

SHAPE: Liquid, which forms a large cloud in the water
COLOR: Green or yellow
SMELL: 3
COOL FACT: Scientists can tell if a shark is stressed by studying its poop.

Great cormorant
Phalacrocorax carbo

SHAPE: Liquid. After it has dried, the poo is called 'guano'.
COLOR: White
SMELL: 3
COOL FACT: When cormorants poop in trees, the acid in their poop kills the leaves.

Earthworm
Lumbricus terrestris

SHAPE: Like muddy soil. A pile of worm poop is called a "cast."
COLOR: Same color as the surrounding soil
SMELL: 1
COOL FACT: An earthworm dumps at least half its own weight in poop every single day.

House mouse
Mus musculus

SHAPE: Small pellets. Fresh poops are hard, but old ones are crumbly.
COLOR: Brown
SMELL: 2
COOL FACT: A house mouse can poop up to 50 times a day.

Domestic chicken
Gallus gallus domesticus

SHAPE: Squidgy balls of poop
COLOR: Brown or dark green, with white areas
SMELL: 2
COOL FACT: Chickens poop over 12 times a day. But when they're sitting on eggs, they take one huge daily poop instead.

Goldfish
Carassius auratus

SHAPE: Fat pellets
COLOR: Varies according to what goldfish eat
SMELL: 1
COOL FACT: Goldfish poop normally sinks to the bottom. (If it doesn't, the fish may be unwell.)

House fly
Musca domestica

SHAPE: Tiny dots stuck to windows and walls
COLOR: Black
SMELL: 1
COOL FACT: Flies poop every time they land. They also poop on their own food.

75

Poo Knew?

Curious to know more? Here are some of the most popular questions about poop...

How big was the biggest human poop?

The biggest human poop that we know of was done by a Viking 1,200 years ago. This colossal poop measures a whopping 8 inches in length and is so old that it has turned into a fossil. You can even see the poop at the Jorvik Viking Centre in York, England.

Why do some poops float and others sink?

Usually, our poop sinks like a stone. That's because human poop is denser (heavier and more compact) than water. But our poop floats if it has lots of fiber, fat, or gas in it.

Back in time, did royalty have their bums wiped for them?

Probably not! However, the Tudor kings of England did employ a Groom of the Stool, who cleaned the king's toilet and helped the king wash. The queens of England had their own female attendants, known as the Ladies of the Bedchamber. It was considered a great honor to hold these positions!

Can poop explode?

Amazingly, poop does blow up occasionally. When it breaks down, or decays, it releases gases. If the poop is in a sealed container (instead of a dog poop bag) and there is no way for the gases to escape, the build-up of gases can eventually cause an explosion. So never store poop like this (unless a doctor asks you to take a sample of poop to them).

Do plants poop?

Well, that depends on what you mean by "poop." Plants do not produce solid poops, but they *do* produce various kinds of waste, including oxygen, gas, and water vapor. Plants also give off methane gas, a substance often found in human and cow farts. So you could say that plants "fart"...

Did people really believe there were gods that pooped gold?

They really did! The Aztecs thought that gold was the poop of various gods, including several sun gods.

Is flamingo poop pink?

No! It's actually gray, brown, or white. But some penguins and whales have pink poop.

How do toilets work on a submarine?

When you flush a toilet on a submarine, the poop and pee goes into a tank. When the tank is full, air is pumped into the tank to blast the contents into the sea.

Which animal has the *stinkiest* poop?

Some people say dog poop smells the worst. Other people think otter, skunk, or snake poop is the stinkiest. There's no "right" answer to this question because everyone has their own opinion.

Is there a word for studying poop?

Yes! In fact, there are *two* words for the study of poop—scatology (*ska–tol–uh–jee*) and coprology (*kop–rol–uh–jee*).

Is it true there are beaches made of poop?

Yes! You can walk on beaches where the white sand is mainly fish poop. The poop comes from parrotfish, which love to munch coral. The parrotfish poop is like white powder, so it creates beautiful beaches!

77

Glossary

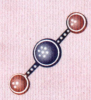
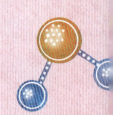

bacteria
Tiny, single-celled life form. Some bacteria can be helpful, but others cause disease.

carbohydrate
A form of sugar made by plants. It is an essential nutrient that provides lots of energy.

carbon dioxide
A gas found in the air. Animals breathe it out, but plants absorb it.

carnivore
A meat-eating animal with teeth for tearing flesh.

constipation
Pooping less often, and it may be hard work. Your poop may also be dry, hard, and lumpy.

contaminated
When something is polluted or dirty.

diarrhea
When your poop is very loose and watery, and you need to visit the bathroom frequently.

digest
To break down food to release its nutrients.

digestive system
The organs that work as a team to break down, or digest, food. They include the mouth, esophagus, stomach, and small and large intestines.

excrement
Another name for poop.

feces
Another name for poop.

fat
An essential nutrient that contains more energy than any other kind of nutrient. Our body uses it to build cells and as fuel.

fertilizer
A substance that is added to soil to help plants grow.

fiber
Tough plant material that our body can't break down or digest, but which is important for a healthy digestive system.

food intolerance
A condition where someone finds it difficult to digest food, and they have an unpleasant reaction to it.

fungi
A large group of living things that includes mushrooms and yeast. There are tiny fungi in our microbiome.

germs
Tiny living things that cause disease, such as bacteria, parasites, and viruses. They live on and inside our bodies. Poop is full of germs.

gut
Another name for the small and large intestines. Its main job is to digest food.

herbivore
A plant-eating animal.

larva
An early stage in the life of various animals, such as insects, before they change into adults.

methane
A gas given off by microbes when they break down plant and animal material. It is also found in farts.

microbe
A tiny living thing too small for us to see with the naked eye.

microbiome
The millions of microbes, including bacteria, fungi, and viruses, that form a vast community in our body.

mineral
A chemical substance, such as iron, which is important for health.

mucus
A type of slimy substance. It covers the insides of the final stages of our digestive system to help the poop slide through them.

nutrient
A substance our body needs for energy or growth.

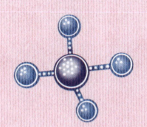

organism
A living thing.

parasite
A living thing found on or inside another living thing, which feeds off it. Parasites are harmful.

protein
An essential nutrient that is needed for growth. Muscle, finger and toe nails, and hair are made mainly of protein.

sewage
Human waste, including poop and pee.

sewer
An underground pipe or channel for carrying sewage.

stool
The medical name for poop, used by doctors and nurses.

virus
A tiny form of life that grows inside the cells of another living thing. Viruses can cause disease.

vitamin
A natural substance found in food that our body cannot make but needs to stay healthy.

weightlessness
The feeling of having little or no weight, which humans experience in space.

Index

Africa 38, 44, 53, 58, 59, 69
air 19, 35, 57, 70
ancient China 28, 43, 68
ancient Egypt 28, 42
ancient Rome 51
animals 6, 28, 31–39, 48, 49, 55–58, 60, 61, 68, 69, 72–75, 77
Antarctica 35
anus 16
Asia 53, 58
astronauts 70, 71
Australia 53
Aztecs 44, 77

bacteria 10, 13, 15, 19, 20, 22, 24, 29, 37, 61, 70
balanced diet 11, 23
Bazalgette, Joseph 51
Belize 45
bile 11
biogas 62
blood 14, 18, 22
Blue Poop Challenge 66, 67
bodies 9–11, 14–16, 17, 22, 24, 25, 38, 63, 66, 70
bowel movement 26
Bristol Stool Scale 26
burps 9, 18, 19

cacosmia 27
camouflage 38, 39
carbohydrates 12, 14
cells 10, 33
Chile 48
climate change 56, 62
colon 15–17, 19
colostomy 16
constipation 27
contamination 25, 50, 60, 61
coprology 77
coprophagy 36
Crapper, Thomas 46
Crete 42
Cumming, Alexander 46

diarrhea 25, 27
digestion 12–14, 19, 22, 32, 37
digestive system 6, 9, 12, 14, 18, 19, 22, 26, 29, 37, 66, 67
diseases 25, 35, 64, 68
doctors 6, 26–28, 64, 67, 68, 76

electricity 6, 55, 62
England 26, 53, 76
Europe 44, 45, 48

farts 9, 18, 19, 76
fats 11, 14, 76
fiber 11, 23, 27, 32, 53, 76
flushing 17, 44–47, 77
food 6, 9, 11–15, 19, 20, 23, 25, 27, 31, 36, 56, 62, 66
France 19
fungi 22, 24

gases 19, 62, 76
Guatemala 45
gut microbiome 22, 23, 67

Harington, Sir John 46
health 11, 16, 20–23, 29, 60

India 42, 58, 59
Indonesia 52
Indus Valley Civilization 42
infections 25, 27, 29, 64, 68
Italy 53

Japan 47, 52, 53

kidneys 18

large intestine 15, 16, 22
larvae 36, 38

Manzoni, Piero 53
Maya 45
medicines 25, 28, 29
Mexico 44, 45, 58
microbes 22, 23, 25, 67
minerals 11, 63
Minoan people 42
mucus 17
muscles 13, 14, 16, 18

Native American peoples 73
North America 48, 73
nutrients 14, 15, 36, 37, 56, 57, 62, 74

Ofili, Chris 53
organs 9, 13, 14, 18

Pakistan 42
parasites 24, 35
Peru 48

poop
  animals' 32–39, 48, 49, 52, 53, 55–58, 61, 62, 68, 69, 72–75, 77
  appearance of 26, 67
  "banks" 29
  changes in 20
  colors of 6, 10, 27
  cures 28, 29
  gods of 6, 45
  going 17, 26
  history of 6, 42–45, 76
  medical term for 26
  names for 6
  pollution 61
  uses of 6, 31, 40, 44, 48–50, 52, 53, 55, 58, 59, 61–63, 71, 73
proteins 11, 14
Pujol, Joseph 19

rectum 16, 17
Romans 18, 28, 44, 45, 51

scatology 77
scientists 6, 20, 22, 29, 31, 33, 35, 63, 64, 66–69, 75
seven signs of life 31
sewage 50, 51, 60, 61, 63
sewers 51, 60
Skara Brae 43
small intestine 13–15, 22
South America 58
South Korea 47
Spain 48
stomach 13–15, 19
stomach bugs 27, 29
Sumerian people 42

toilets 17, 25, 26, 33, 40, 42–47, 71, 76, 77
Turkey 58

vets 64
viruses 22, 24, 61

washing hands 24, 25
waste 9, 10, 15–18, 31–33, 35, 36, 38, 40, 42–44, 46, 49, 50, 51, 57, 60–62, 71, 76
water 10, 15, 18, 24, 25, 27, 42, 44–47, 50, 56, 58–61, 63, 69, 71, 75, 76
pee (urine) 9, 10, 18, 32, 39, 50, 70, 71, 73, 77